CW00369900

Religion

London: H M S O

Researched and written by Reference Services, Central Office of Information.

© Crown copyright 1992
Applications for reproduction should be made to HMSO.
First published 1992

ISBN 0 11 701665 9

HMSO publications are available from:

HMSO Publications Centre
(Mail, fax and telephone orders only)
PO Box 276, London SW8 5DT
Telephone orders 071-873 9090
General enquiries 071-873 0011
(queuing system in operation for both numbers)
Fax orders 071-873 8200

HMSO Bookshops
49 High Holborn, London WC1V 6HB
071-873 0011 Fax 071-873 8200 (counter service only)
258 Broad Street, Birmingham B1 2HE
021-643 3740 Fax 021-643 6510
Southey House, 33 Wine Street, Bristol BS1 2BQ
0272 264306 Fax 0272 294515
9-21 Princess Street, Manchester M60 8AS
061-834 7201 Fax 061-833 0634
16 Arthur Street, Belfast BT1 4GD
0232 238451 Fax 0232 235401
71 Lothian Road, Edinburgh EH3 9AZ
031-228 4181 Fax 031-229 2734

HMSO's Accredited Agents
(see Yellow Pages)

and through good booksellers

Photo Credits
Numbers refer to the pages of the illustration section (1–8): Scotsman Publications p. 1 (top); Tomas Jaski Ltd p. 1 (bottom); Hutchison p. 2 (top), p. 7 (bottom); Universal Pictorial p. 2 (bottom); Rex Features p. 3 (top), p. 6 (top), p. 7 (top), p. 8 (top left); Council of Churches for Britain and Ireland p. 3 (bottom); Salvation Army p. 4 (top); Methodist Church p. 4 (bottom); Jon Walter p. 5 (top); Michael Morris p. 5 (bottom); Crown Copyright p. 6 (bottom); Leicester City Council p. 8 (top right); *The Times*, London p. 8 (bottom).

Contents

Introduction

Most of the world's religions are represented in contemporary Britain.[1] This book, as part of the *Aspects of Britain* series, seeks to describe the main churches and religious communities active in Britain, focusing on their origins, their development within Britain and their organisation. The book also outlines the limited role played by the state in religious affairs.

Although Britain has been predominantly Christian since Saxon times, following the Reformation in the sixteenth century many different Christian denominations have existed. Most of the Christian churches active in other countries are represented in Britain. At the same time many British churches are actively involved in Christian missionary work overseas, and many of the churches founded in Britain are now well-established in other countries as a result both of conversions and of the settlement of British immigrants.

Most of those in Britain who adhere to non-Christian religions belong to communities which originally came from other countries. Of these the Jewish community is of the longest standing: the origins of the present community can be traced back to the seventeenth century. Since the 1950s immigration from

---

[1] The term 'Britain' is used in this book to mean the United Kingdom of Great Britain and Northern Ireland; 'Great Britain' comprises England, Wales and Scotland.

the countries of the Commonwealth has brought hundreds of thousands of Hindus, Muslims and Sikhs to Britain.

There have also been a number of British converts to the main non-Christian religions. The Buddhist community in Britain is largely made up of people of British or Western origin who have converted to Buddhism: only a minority of British Buddhists come from traditionally Buddhist countries.

Such trends have contributed to the religious diversity of contemporary Britain. In addition to the main religions and Christian denominations, there has also been considerable interest in alternative religions and related movements. This is reflected in the large variety of new religious cults, many of which incorporate elements of existing mainstream religions, and in the growth of the New Age movement. There are also many informal Christian groups which are only loosely connected, if at all, with the main churches. Non-religious alternatives are offered by organisations such as the British Humanist Association and the National Secular Society.

The book also covers the separate religious traditions which have developed in Scotland, which, along with England, is the only part of Britain to have its own established church. In Northern Ireland and Wales, there are churches, formerly established, which maintain links with the Church of England (see p. 26); in addition to some of the main churches and religious groups found elsewhere in Britain, there are also a number of locally-based Protestant denominations.

Religion and National Life

Everyone in Britain has the right to religious freedom (in teaching, worship and observance) without interference from the community or the State. Religious organisations and groups may own property, run schools, and promote their beliefs in speech and writing. There is no religious bar to the holding of public office, although clergy of the Church of England (together with those of the Church of Scotland, the Church of Ireland and the Roman Catholic Church) are not allowed to sit in the House of Commons.

Religious Tolerance

Britain has a long tradition of religious tolerance, and the past 30 years have seen the acceptance of the wide variety of religious beliefs and traditions of the large numbers of immigrants of different nationalities, although immigrants also belong to Britain's existing Christian denominations. The ethnic minority population now totals about 2.58 million—some 4.7 per cent of the total population—of whom about 45 per cent were born in Britain.

Freedom of conscience in religious matters in Britain was achieved gradually from the seventeenth century onwards. The laws discriminating against minority religious groups were gradually administered less harshly and then finally repealed. Heresy ceased to be a legal offence with the passage of the Ecclesiastical Jurisdiction Act 1677, and the Toleration Act 1688 granted freedom of worship to Protestant minority groups. In 1828 the repeal of the Test and Corporation Acts gave Nonconformists (see p. 32) full political rights, making it possible for them to be appointed to public office; in 1835 they were accorded similar rights in municipal government. Roman Catholics gained political rights under the Roman Catholic Relief Act 1829, and the Jewish Relief Act 1858 enabled Jews to become Members of Parliament. In addition, the religious tests imposed on prospective students and academic staff of the universities of Oxford, Cambridge and Durham were successively abolished by Acts of 1854, 1856 and 1871. Similar restrictions on the staff of Scottish universities were formally removed in 1932.

During the nineteenth century the Church of England lost many of its privileges as a state religion, with the commutation of church tithes (a tax paid to the church) in 1836; the introduction of civil registration of births, marriages and deaths in 1836 (today almost half of all marriages are civil ceremonies); and the abolition of the compulsory church rate (money raised from parishioners for the repair of church buildings) in 1868. In 1936 it was announced that commuted tithes would be replaced with redemption annuities, payable until 1996, by which time all tithes, with minor exceptions, would be abolished. In practice almost all tithe payments have already ceased.

The Established Churches

There are two established churches in Britain, that is, churches legally recognised as official churches of the State: in England the (Anglican) Church of England, of which the Sovereign is the Supreme Governor; and in Scotland the (Presbyterian) Church of Scotland.

The special status of the Church of England is reflected in the fact that the Church's two archbishops (of Canterbury and York), the bishops of London, Durham and Winchester, and 21 other bishops (according to their seniority as diocesan bishops) sit, by virtue of their positions, in the House of Lords. Bishops of the Church of Ireland ceased to sit in the Lords in 1871 following the disestablishment of their church, and Welsh bishops ceased to sit in 1920 following the disestablishment of their church. (A number of other religious leaders have been granted life peerages. These include Lord Jakobovits, the former Chief Rabbi, and Lord Soper, the former President of the Methodist Conference. Former Archbishops of Canterbury, including Lord Coggan and Lord Runcie, have also been granted life peerages.) Ministers of the established churches, as well as those belonging to other religious communities, work in services run by the State, such as the armed forces and national hospitals, and are paid a salary for such services by the state. In prisons Anglican, Church of Scotland, Roman Catholic and Methodist chaplains provide opportunities for worship and spiritual counselling. They are supported by visiting ministers of other denominations and faiths as required.

State Financial Assistance

The State makes no direct contribution to the expenses of religious groups. However, since 1977 limited state aid has been given for the repair of historic churches; in 1990–91 English Heritage grants to churches totalled £8.2 million. In April 1991 the Government announced that £11.5 million of new money would be made available to assist with the costs of repairs to cathedrals and comparable buildings over the following three years. Such funding is not restricted to Church of England buildings (although in practice most of the oldest church buildings belong to the Church of England—see pp. 18 and 32). The first grants awarded by English Heritage were announced in October 1991.

The Government also contributes towards the Redundant Churches Fund, a body which maintains some 270 redundant Church of England churches for which no alternative use can be found but which are of architectural or historic importance. The contribution for the period 1989 to 1994 will be about £8.7 million.

Religious organisations can normally obtain charitable status and as a result benefit from tax relief.

Religious Involvement in Social Issues

The main Christian churches and many other religious groups are closely involved in the work of a wide range of charities and voluntary organisations which seek to meet specific social needs.

The churches' involvement in broader social issues was highlighted in the Church of England report *Faith in the City: A Call for Action by Church and Nation*, published in 1985. This made recommendations for improving conditions in the inner cities and other socially deprived areas and led to the establishment in 1988 of the Church of England's Church Urban Fund, which aims to raise money for the Church's work in inner city and other priority areas. By the end of 1991 it had raised more than £21.3 million and given grants to 451 inner city projects. The Department of the Environment has offered to help in evaluating the performance of the fund. Two further reports, *Living Faith in the City* and *Faith in the Countryside*, were published in 1990.

The establishment of an Inner Cities Religious Council, to meet regularly and discuss the full range of issues affecting urban areas, was announced in November 1991. It is chaired by a minister at the Department of the Environment and includes representatives of the Church of England, the Roman Catholic Church, the Free Church Federal Council, the black-led churches and the Hindu, Jewish, Muslim and Sikh faiths. A clergyman working for the Church of England's Board for Social Responsibility has been seconded to the Department of Environment's Inner Cities Directorate.

Other religious groups attach great importance to social affairs. The Free Church Federal Council (see p. 32) includes concern for social issues among its activities; its Moderator is patron of a wide range of organisations which are active in the social field. The Roman Catholic Bishops' Conference of England and Wales (see p. 41) includes a Department for Christian Responsibility and Citizenship which has committees covering, among other things, social welfare and community relations. Organisations belonging to other religious communities are concerned with a range of social issues (see, for example, pp. 51 and 54).

In Scotland there is a similar tradition of involvement; the Church and Nation Committee of the General Assembly of the Church of Scotland plays a prominent part in the discussion of such issues.

Statistics on Religious Affiliation

There is no standard information about the number of members of religious groups since questions are not normally asked about religious beliefs in censuses or for other official purposes, except in Northern Ireland. The only national Census of Attendance at Religious Worship was in 1851, although in recent times a number of attempts have been made to estimate the size of the different religious communities. Religious groups adopt their own ways of counting their members, and membership figures are therefore approximate.

There has been a fall in recent years in both the number of full-time ministers and the number of adults recorded as members of most of the larger Christian churches. At the same time there has been significant growth in a range of independent, Afro-Caribbean and Pentecostalist churches, and in new religious movements.

Recent surveys suggest that about 10 per cent of the adult population of Britain regularly attend church, as compared with 4 per cent of the adult population in Denmark, 13 per cent in France, 14 per cent in Spain, 27 per cent in Australia and 40 per cent in the USA. Sixty-five per cent of people in Britain identify, to some degree, with a Christian church.

A survey in 1989 estimated that there were 38,607 Christian churches or congregations in Britain—one for every 1,200 people, and that the number of churches had declined slightly since 1979.

A number of surveys in recent years have revealed more general evidence about people's beliefs and attitudes to religion. According to the results of one survey, published in 1991, 54 per cent of the population of Britain claimed to be religious and 71 per cent said they believe in God. Twenty-five per cent retained a Christian belief in hell and 44 per cent said they believed in life after death. Sixty-five per cent said it was important to have a religious service following the birth of a child, 79 per cent said it was important for a marriage and 84 per cent for a death.

Education

Religious education in publicly maintained schools is required by law in England and Wales, and, together with the National Curriculum, forms part of the basic curriculum for all pupils. In county schools (schools provided and maintained by local authorities out of public funds) religious education must be non-denominational and must be provided in accordance with a locally-agreed syllabus. The Education Reform Act 1988 requires all new syllabuses to reflect the fact that the religious traditions in Britain are in the main Christian, whilst taking account of the teaching and practices of the other principal religions represented in the country.

Voluntary schools include voluntary-aided, voluntary-controlled and special agreement schools. They are largely established by religious denominations and comprise about one-third of all schools. Voluntary-aided and special agreement schools contribute 15 per cent towards the capital cost of establishing such schools and the responsibility for maintenance is shared between governors and the local education authority. Voluntary-controlled schools are usually wholly maintained from public funds and in some cases the local education authority will also cover the capital costs of establishing the school. In voluntary schools religious education must generally be provided in accordance with the school's trust deed.

Schools also have to provide a daily act of *collective worship*. In county schools collective worship must be wholly or mainly of a broadly Christian character. The law provides for the lifting of this requirement if the head-teacher considers it inappropriate for some or all pupils. Where an application to lift the broadly Christian requirement has been granted, worship must still be provided for the pupils concerned. If the application applies to a group of pupils from different faith backgrounds, worship in which all can participate may be held, for example using themes common to several religions. Alternatively, if the pupils all come from the same faith background, single-faith worship may be provided for them. Parents may withdraw their children from both religious education and collective worship if they wish.

In *Scotland* the Education (Scotland) Act 1980 imposes similar requirements. Scottish education authorities are required to see that schools practise religious observance and give pupils religious instruction; parents may withdraw their children if they wish. Guidance has been issued to education authorities recommending that religious education and observance in schools should be based on Christianity while promoting understanding of, and respect for, those who belong to different faiths. Certain schools provide for Roman Catholic children but in all schools there are safeguards for the individual conscience.

In *Northern Ireland* all schools must be open to pupils of all religions, although most Catholic pupils attend Catholic schools and most Protestant children are enrolled at local authority schools. The policy of successive governments has been to encourage integrated education, providing for both Protestant and Roman Catholic pupils, where there is a local desire for it: new integrated schools receive immediate government funding.

Schools in Northern Ireland are obliged to offer religious education and collective worship, although parents have the right to withdraw their children from both. In controlled schools clergy have a right of access which may be used for denominational instruction. In voluntary schools collective worship and religious education are controlled by the management authorities.

The Education Act 1980 gives parents a statutory right to express views about the school they would like their children to attend, and local authorities are under a duty to meet the parents' wishes. The Education Reform Act 1988 requires schools to admit pupils up to the limit of their physical capacity. These Acts provide, for example, a stronger basis for those parents seeking admission for their children to single-sex schools; they also make it easier for families in areas where there are no such schools to apply to schools in neighbouring authorities' areas. The 1988 Education Reform Act also established new arrangements for schools to withdraw from local authority control and to be directly funded as grant-maintained schools, subject to ballots of the governors and parents and the approval of the Secretary of State. While the school has to be of the same character as before it acquired grant-maintained status, there is provision for changing its character subject to permission from the Secretary of State for Education.

Different religious groups have established a large number of private, fee-paying schools. These can apply for voluntary-aided status, whereby the State would meet all running costs and most capital costs while the founders would continue to be in a majority on the schools' governing bodies.

Religious studies and theology are taught at a wide variety of universities and colleges; many religious bodies also run their own colleges to train men and women to officiate at their services and carry out other duties.

Broadcasting

Although there is no obligation for the British Broadcasting Corporation (BBC) to show religious programmes, the BBC has, since its foundation, broadcast religious programmes on both radio and television. These include *Thought for the Day* on Radio Four's *Today* programme and *Everyman* on BBC1. BBC Television's Religious Programmes Department produces about 150 hours of television a year (this amounts to about two per cent of television output and about two per cent of the total BBC television budget). It seeks to reflect all the faiths active in Britain through broadcast worship, study programmes and documentaries.

The Broadcasting Act 1990 allows Christian and other religious groups to compete for licences to have their own local radio stations. They can also seek licences for radio broadcasts (of short duration and covering limited geographical areas) and licences for some cable and satellite television channels. The Act also requires those running television stations on the new Channel 3 service (which will replace the independent television system from January 1993) to provide sufficent time for religious programmes. Such broadcasting will be expected to recognise the range of religious beliefs in Britain. The new Channel 5 service will also be required to include religious programmes.

The Act also requires the Independent Television Commission and the Radio Authority (the bodies responsible for licensing and regulating independent broadcasting) to publish guidance on their criteria for deciding whether any religious group may be disqualified as programme providers and from holding satellite, cable or radio licences; no religious group is permitted to hold a national radio licence. Religious programmes are not allowed to exploit their audiences improperly, nor to abuse the religious views of others.

Radio and television organisations broadcast programmes of special interest to ethnic minorities, including programmes of a religious nature. The Asian Programmes Unit of the BBC produces a variety of programmes on Asian themes. Several of the independent television companies run magazine programmes for minority groups, and Channel 4 transmits a regular current affairs programme for ethnic minorities. Channel 4 has broadcast programmes on such subjects as Sufism (see p. 54), the Hindu festival of Durga Puja and the role of the black churches in Britain. BBC and independent local radio stations serving areas with significant minority populations broadcast news, magazine and music programmes for ethnic minorities, including items of religious interest.

In 1988 a survey found that over 60 per cent of the population watched a religious programme on television at least once a month.

Advertising

The Broadcasting Act 1990 requires the broadcasting authorities to establish guidelines on advertising. Guidelines issued by the Radio Authority allow religious groups to advertise on radio provided the advertisements do not seek to recruit people to a particular faith or belief. Groups which advocate illegal behaviour are not allowed to advertise. Fund-raising is permitted only by groups with charitable status and on the condition that it does not involve 'improper exploitation of any susceptibilities of those listening'. Religious groups may also sponsor programmes. Religious advertising is banned on Independent Television,

Channel 4 and some satellite services until the end of 1992. On the other services such advertising is allowed provided it complies with the guidelines issued by the Independent Television Commission.

Religious Observance at Work

Religious observance at places of work may present difficulties for employers and employees where production processes are involved—for example, Muslims are obliged to pray five times a day at set times, while the Islamic festivals of Id al Fitr and Id al Adha are marked by communal prayers. The Commission for Racial Equality has emphasised the need for arrangements to make possible the religious practices of employees as a means of assuring harmonious working relations and uninterrupted production. Its Code of Practice in Employment, which came into force in 1984, includes guidance for employers on such matters and recommends that employers should consider how work requirements can be adapted to meet religious and cultural needs. The Department of Employment's Race Relations Employment Advisory Service provides guidance to employers and others on equal-opportunity policies which help to ensure equal opportunity in employment, irrespective of race, colour, nationality or ethnic or national origin. Advisers seek to bring about change and give advice on the Race Relations Act 1976 and the Commission for Racial Equality's Code of Practice.

The Law of Blasphemy

The law of blasphemy in England and Wales applies only to the Christian religion, and in particular to the doctrines of the Church of England. The law has been reviewed by the Law Commission, whose report, *Offences against Religion and Public Worship*, was published in 1985. A majority of the Commissioners recommended that existing offences should be abolished and not replaced; however a minority proposed the creation of a new statutory offence curbing the publication of 'grossly abusive or insulting material relating to a religion with the purpose of wounding or outraging religious feelings' which would cover religions generally. A group established by the Archbishop of Canterbury to consider the Law Commission's findings reported in 1988 and expressed agreement with the dissenting Law Commissioners. The Government has taken the view that there is not sufficient agreement in favour of change to justify an amendment to the law. It considers that there would be immense difficulties over defining what should or should not be blasphemous. It also believes that it would be difficult to decide whether all faiths, including the very minor and obscure, should be protected, and that an alteration in the law could lead to litigation which would damage relations between faiths.

In practice the law is little used and there has been no successful public prosecution for blasphemy since 1921; the only successful private prosecution since then was in 1977.

The Church of England

Origins of Christianity in England

During the period of Roman rule (AD 43–408) the religion of Rome and the religion of the indigenous Celts existed side by side. The religion of the Celts was under the leadership of druids; there is some evidence of links with druids elsewhere in Europe.

Roman rule led to the introduction of a number of different religions practised in different parts of the Roman empire. It is possible that Christianity first arrived in England in this way in the second century AD. A definite sign of its development was the attendance of three British bishops and a deacon at the Church Council of Arles in 314.

The development of Christianity was halted by the Saxon invasions, although in parts of the north and west of the country it never entirely died out, but operated as an independent Celtic Church. The continuous history of the Church of England dates from its foundation by St Augustine in 597. Augustine (d. 604) was a monk sent by the Pope to convert the English. He successfully began to introduce the Roman Catholic Church into England; the independence of the Celtic Church was virtually ended at the Synod of Whitby in 664. By the time of the Norman Conquest in 1066 the Roman Catholic Church was universally accepted in England.

Throughout the middle ages the Church remained part of the Roman Catholic Church, subject to the authority of the Pope. The most notable dissenters in England were the Lollards, the group of wandering preachers inspired by John Wycliff, an Oxford theologian and priest (d. 1384). The Lollards rejected many of the doctrines of the Roman Catholic Church and, as a result, were subjected to persecution. Their ideas foreshadowed much of the thinking of the Protestant Reformation. Wycliff was also involved in preparing the first complete English translation of the Bible; the translation of the Bible into English was not officially approved until the 1530s.

The Reformation

The Protestant Reformation originated, in the main, on the continent of Europe. At first its impact on England was limited. When King Henry VIII (1509–47) asserted the independence of the Church of England from the authority of the Pope in 1534 he did so largely for personal and political reasons; he had no wish to set up a reformed church. Although Henry became 'supreme head, next under Christ, of the Church of England' (a title later modified to 'Supreme Governor') and dissolved the monasteries, much Catholic doctrine remained intact.

Under Henry's son and successor, King Edward VI (1547–53), the Church of England became more Protestant. Edward was succeeded by his half-sister Queen Mary (1553–58), who attempted to restore Roman Catholicism. Queen Mary's successor, her half-sister Queen Elizabeth I (1558–1603), sought to impose a degree of national uniformity based on a religious compromise. The Elizabethan Settlement is commonly regarded as the origin of the Church of England in its current form; it was expressed in the Act of Uniformity 1559 and the Act of

Supremacy 1559. Doctrine was set out in the Thirty-Nine Articles which achieved their final form in 1571.

As a result of this compromise the Church of England (or Anglican Church) has always included a wide variety of beliefs, opinions and forms of worship, ranging from a 'High Church' or Catholic position to a 'Low Church' Protestant or Evangelical position. The translation of the Bible authorised by King James I in 1611 is still in use today, alongside newer translations. The only interruption in the subsequent history of the Church of England was during the period of the Commonwealth (1649–60) which followed the English Civil War, when the established church was for a time nominally Presbyterian and a number of dissenting Protestant groups enjoyed considerable success.

For historical reasons, nearly all the oldest churches in England belong to the Church of England, since at the time of the Reformation all the country's churches and cathedrals became its property. It has been estimated that just over half the Anglican churches were built before 1500.

The Church's Relationship with the State

As the established Church in England (see p. 4), the Church's relationship with the State is one of mutual obligation—the Church's privileges are balanced by certain duties it must fulfil. As the Supreme Governor of the Church of England the Sovereign must always be a member of the Church, and promise to uphold it; the succession is restricted to Protestants, and those who marry Roman Catholics are excluded, although their children remain eligible. The Sovereign is crowned by the Archbishop of Canterbury, who holds an important office of the State. The Archbishop also traditionally baptises, and conducts the wedding ceremonies of, close members of the royal family. He also preaches on state occasions in Westminster Abbey or at St Paul's Cathedral. He and other senior members of the Church of England have seats in the House of Lords (see p. 5) and in the official order of precedence he stands above the Prime Minister: only the Sovereign and his or her immediate family rank above him. The position of Archbishop gives the holder considerable opportunities to make a contribution to public affairs.

The Church of England's public worship is governed by law; the forms of worship currently approved are the Book of Common Prayer of 1662 (which is approved indefinitely) and the Alternative Service Book of 1980, which is authorised until 2000.

The Sovereign is served by the Ecclesiastical Household which includes the Clerk of the Closet, usually a bishop, whose traditional duty was 'to attend at the right hand of the Sovereign in the Royal Closet during Divine Service to resolve such doubts as may arise concerning spiritual matters'. It also includes the Dean and Sub-Dean of the Chapels Royal, who exercise jurisdiction over the chapels royal in England. (A chapel royal is a chapel attached to the Court which is not subject to the jurisdiction of a bishop.) There are chapels royal at St James's Palace, Hampton Court Palace and the Tower of London. The Sovereign is also served by domestic chaplains and chaplains-in-ordinary; the latter also have a rota of attendance to conduct divine service and preach at chapels royal.

Church Appointments

Church of England archbishops, bishops and deans of cathedrals (but not provosts—see below) are appointed by the Sovereign on the advice of the Prime Minister, and all clergy swear their allegiance to the Sovereign. The Crown Appointments Commission, set up in 1977, plays a decisive part in the selection of archbishops and diocesan bishops. The Commission consists of six members elected by the General Synod (see below): three from the House of Clergy and three from the House of Laity, the Archbishops of Canterbury and York, four people chosen by the vacant diocese, and two non-voting members—the Prime Minister's appointments secretary and the Archbishops' appointments secretary. It submits a shortlist of two candidates, normally in order of preference, to the Prime Minister. The Prime Minister may select either name or ask for a further name or names from which to make a recommendation to the Sovereign to appoint. When the See of Canterbury is vacant the Prime Minister appoints the Chairman of the Crown Appointments Commission.

Appointments are confirmed by a secret ballot of the chapter (the dean, or provost, and canons—see below) of the cathedral concerned, although by tradition this is a formality. Suffragan bishops, who share the ministry of diocesan bishops, are appointed by the Sovereign on the recommendation of the diocesan bishop concerned; two names are submitted to the Prime Minister who by custom and practice recommends the first to the Sovereign. The Prime Minister also advises the Sovereign on the appointment of clergy to a large number of livings (or church positions) where the right of appointment is traditionally held by the Crown.

Structure
The Church has two provinces: Canterbury, comprising 30 dioceses (including the Diocese of Europe), and York, which has 14 dioceses. The Archbishop of Canterbury is 'Primate of All

England', and the Archbishop of York 'Primate of England'. The dioceses are headed by bishops, often assisted by suffragan bishops, who share responsibility for part of the diocese's ministry, either on a geographical basis or for particular activities. The title 'bishop', derived from the Greek *episkopos* (an overseer), refers to a clergyman consecrated as ecclesiastical governor of a diocese and possessing powers of confirming, instituting and ordaining. Archdeacons exercise administrative authority and pastoral care over all or part of a diocese under the authority of the diocesan bishop.

Cathedrals are the responsibility of the *dean* (or *provost* in the case of cathedrals which are also parish churches). The chapter includes residentiary *canons*, who are senior clergymen on the cathedral staff. Honorary canons are appointed to mark distinguished ministry in other roles in a diocese. Canons may also retain the ancient title of *prebendary*.

Dioceses are divided into deaneries. These are in turn divided into a total of over 13,000 parishes, although increasingly two or more parishes are combined and are served by a number of clergymen operating as a team or group ministry.

There are altogether 10,500 ordained stipendiary Church of England priests, and 600 stipendiary women deacons.

Each of the two provinces has its own *Convocation* (or assembly), consisting of an Upper House of diocesan bishops and elected suffragan bishops and a Lower House of *ex officio* and elected clergy.

General Synod

The central governing body of the Church of England is the General Synod, which was inaugurated by the Queen in 1970, replacing the former Church Assembly. The General Synod's measures must be approved by Parliament where they are considered by the Ecclesiastical Committee which consists of 15 Members of Parliament (MPs) and 15 peers.

The total membership of the General Synod is 560, divided into three houses—bishops, clergy and laity. All diocesan bishops are members as are nine elected suffragan bishops, while the clergy representatives consist of the lower houses of the two Convocations (see above). The laity representatives are voted for by the laity members of the deanery synods which are in turn elected by parochial church councils. These are elected by people on each parish's electoral register. The General Synod must meet at least twice a year. Some important issues are referred to the approval of the dioceses before being decided by the Synod. Lay people are also involved in church government in the parishes, both through the ancient office of church-warden and through membership of modern parochial church councils.

The General Synod's permanent staff is headed by the Secretary-General who is at the centre of an administrative system dealing with such matters as missionary work, inter-church relations, social questions, and recruitment and training for the ministry. This includes theological colleges which train candidates for ordination; other colleges offer part-time courses. The Synod's responsibilities also cover church work in Britain and overseas, the care of church buildings, church schools (which are maintained from public funds—see p. 9), colleges of education, and centres for training women in pastoral work.

Ordination of Women

At present, only men may join the priesthood, but in 1987 the General Synod voted to proceed with legislation to enable women to become priests; final decisions on the matter, however, are not expected to be taken until late 1992 or 1993. The Deacons (Ordination of Women) Measure 1986 has made it possible for women to become deacons. As deacons women can, for example, conduct marriage ceremonies. Women have already been ordained to the priesthood in other parts of the Anglican Communion (see p. 25).

Church Courts

Ecclesiastical law consists of parts of the old canon law which remained in force after the Reformation in the sixteenth century, together with the post-Reformation statutes and canons passed by Parliament and the General Synod. The Church has its own courts, whose jurisdiction today extends only to church property and matters of ecclesiastical discipline. They include Diocesan or Consistory Courts, Provincial Courts, and, for both provinces, the Court of Ecclesiastical Causes Reserved and the Commission of Review. The courts are largely regulated by the Ecclesiastical Jurisdiction Measure 1963. In some cases appeal is to the Judicial Committee of the Privy Council.[2]

Finance

The Church's investment income is managed mainly by the Church Commissioners, who are wholly responsible for the

[2]For further details, see *The British System of Government* (Aspects of Britain: HMSO, 1992).

payment of clergy pensions and provide about 40 per cent of the cost of clergy stipends and housing. Most of the remainder is provided by local voluntary donations. These are also used to maintain and run church buildings. The remainder is passed to dioceses who in turn make contributions to a central fund which finances central services, including training for ordination.

The average stipend of a clergyman is about £12,800; the average value of additional benefits, including free accommodation and a non-contributory pension, is estimated to be £7,260. The stipends for senior figures in the Church are:

	£
Archbishop of Canterbury	43,500
Archbishop of York	38,150
Bishop of London	35,560
Bishop of Durham	31,380
Bishop of Winchester	26,160
Other diocesan bishops	23,610
Suffragan bishops	19,410
Deans and provosts	19,410
Archdeacons	18,300–19,300
Residentiary canons	15,870

The Commissioners' activities are governed by Acts of Parliament and Measures of the General Synod and they report to both Parliament and the General Synod. A Second Church Estates Commissioner, an MP, represents the Commissioners in the House of Commons and answers MPs' questions.

Statistics of Membership

In 1989 it was estimated that, in the two provinces (excluding the Diocese of Europe), some 233,000 people were baptised into the Church; of these 186,000 were under one year old (28.5 per cent of live births). In the same year there were 61,656 confirmations. Attendances at services on a normal Sunday are around 1.2 million, out of a total attendance at Christian churches of about 3.7 million. In 1989, according to figures published by the Office of Population Censuses and Surveys, 118,956 marriages were solemnized in the Church of England and the Church in Wales. These accounted for 66.1 per cent of all marriages with religious ceremonies, and 34.3 per cent of all marriages in England and Wales.

Many people who rarely, if ever, attend services (amounting to perhaps half the population) still regard themselves as belonging to the Church of England.

The Media

Church of England services (along with the services of other denominations) are frequently broadcast on radio and television. Anglican publications include the *Church Times*, an independent weekly newspaper, and the *Church of England Newspaper*, also published on a weekly basis. The Church appoints diocesan communication officers and others who act as a point of contact with the media.

The Anglican Communion

The Anglican Communion comprises 28 autonomous provinces in Britain and overseas and three regional councils overseas with a local membership of about 70 million. In the British Isles there are four provinces: the Church of England (established), the Church in Wales (disestablished in 1920), the Scottish Episcopal Church in Scotland (see p. 29), and the Church of Ireland (disestablished in 1870).

The history of the Church in Wales can be traced back to the founding of the Celtic Church in Wales by native saints, such as St David and St Beuno, in the fifth and sixth centuries. The Church was later reorganised within the Western European Church, becoming part of the Anglican Church at the time of Reformation. (The Bible was translated into Welsh by Bishop Morgan in 1588.)

The disestablishment of the Church in Wales reflected the strength of the Free Churches in Wales. The Church in Wales is an autonomous province of six sees and elects its own bishops. One of the six bishops is elected Archbishop by an electoral college comprising elected lay and clerical members. The Church's governing body consists of three orders—bishops, clergy and laity and has 345 members. It meets twice a year. The church has 116,000 members, 761 clergymen and 1,400 places of worship, including the country's medieval churches and cathedrals.

The Church of Ireland draws most of its membership from people of English descent; the Reformation had little support among the indigenous population of Ireland. It is divided into two provinces, covering both the Irish Republic and Northern Ireland. The Archbishop of Armagh, whose seat is in Northern Ireland, is Primate of All Ireland. The Church of Ireland maintains statistics for the whole of Ireland. In the Irish Republic and Northern Ireland there are altogether about 400,000 members, 650 clergymen and 1,200 places of worship.

The *Lambeth Conference* has met for consultation among all Anglican bishops about every ten years since 1867: the last conference was held in Canterbury in 1988. Presided over by the Archbishop of Canterbury, the Conference has no executive authority, but enjoys considerable influence on matters of doctrine, discipline, relations with other communions, and attitudes to political and social questions. The *Anglican Consultative Council* (an assembly of laypeople and clergy as well as of bishops) meets every two or three years and is intended to allow consultations within the Anglican communion. The Council last met in Wales in 1990.

Religion in Scotland

History

Although most of the religious groups described in the other chapters in this booklet are represented in Scotland, the main Protestant churches in Scotland are distinct from those in England and Wales. This stems from the fact that at the time of the Reformation Scotland was a separate kingdom; as a result the Reformation took a different course in Scotland from that taken in the rest of Britain.

Christianity first reached Scotland in about AD 400. Under the influence of St Columba, who established a Christian community on the island of Iona in 563, it developed as a branch of the Celtic Church (see p. 16) with its own form of worship. Scotland adapted only gradually to the normal ecclesiastical pattern of Western Europe.

Protestantism first appeared in Scotland in 1539 and had only limited support, until the Reformation was imposed by the Scottish Parliament in 1560. Calvinism (based on the teachings of the Geneva-based Protestant reformer John Calvin 1509–64), promoted by such local leaders as John Knox, was much more influential in Scotland than in England. During the late sixteenth century the Presbyterian church order, based on presbyteries or church courts of ministers and elders (all of equal rank) supervising a group of parishes, replaced the bishoprics. (The word 'presbyterian' is derived from the Greek '*presbuteros*', meaning 'elder'.)

In the seventeenth century there were several attempts to make the Scottish church conform to the pattern of the Church of England. However, attempts to reappoint bishops failed and with the 1690 Act of Settlement the Presbyterian order became permanent in the established church (see p. 30).

The relatively small *Episcopal Church of Scotland*, with 61,000 members, was founded after the Act of Settlement. It remains part of the Anglican Communion (see p. 25) but is autonomous. It continues to appoint bishops who choose one of their number as presiding bishop. The governing authority is the General Synod, with 160 elected members, which meets once a year. There are seven bishops, 280 clergy and 341 churches or places of worship.

During the eighteenth century a large number of evangelical dissenters broke away from the Church of Scotland, and in the 'Disruption' of 1843 over a third of the ministers, led by Thomas Chalmers, left to create the Free Church of Scotland. The reunions of 1900 and 1929 brought back most of the dissenters to form the present Church of Scotland, but also left a number of Free Presbyterian churches outside the established church.

Roman Catholicism (see p. 40) never died out in the remoter highland and island regions of Scotland, but most Catholics in present-day Scotland are of Irish descent, their ancestors having arrived in Scotland in the early nineteenth century. Since the eighteenth century a number of other Christian denominations of English origin have been active in Scotland. The oldest non-Christian group in Scotland is the Jewish community, but other groups have become established following the arrival of immigrants of different nationalities.

The Church of Scotland

The Church of Scotland became the national church following the Scottish Reformation; this was consolidated in the Treaty of Union 1707 and the Church of Scotland Act 1921, the latter confirming its complete freedom in all spiritual matters. The Church appoints its own office bearers and its decisions on its affairs are not subject to any civil authority.

Both men and women may join the ministry (women have been ordained as elders since 1966 and as ministers since 1968). There are 1,250 ministers. Each of 1,700 churches is governed locally by the Kirk Session, consisting of the minister and the elected elders of the Church. The elders run parish committees and have an important say in the appointment of ministers. The adult communicant membership of the Church of Scotland is about 790,000, making it the largest church in Scotland.

Above the Kirk Session is the Court of the Presbytery (of which there are 46), then the Court of the Synod (of which there are twelve), and finally the General Assembly, consisting of 1,264 elected ministers and elders, who have the title of commissioner. This meets annually in Edinburgh under the presidency of an elected moderator, who serves for one year. The Sovereign is represented at the General Assembly by the Lord High Commissioner, who ranks next in precedence to the Queen in Scotland while the General Assembly is in session; the Lord Commissioner's expenses (£76,000 in 1991–92) are met out of public funds. The Queen has also attended the General Assembly in person.

There is a chapel royal (see p. 19) at the Palace of Holyroodhouse in Edinburgh.

Other Presbyterian Churches

Smaller, conservative Presbyterian churches include the Free Church of Scotland (often known as the 'Wee Frees'), which represents the minority who did not take part in the 1900 reunion of churches (see p. 29); the Reformed Presbyterian Church of Scotland; and the Free Presbyterian Church, which broke away from the Free Church in 1893 for doctrinal reasons. Most adherents are in the Western Highlands and Islands. The United Free Church is more widely spread geographically.

The Free Churches

The term 'Free Churches' is often used to describe those Protestant churches in Britain which, unlike the Church of England and the Church of Scotland, are not official or established churches. Their members have also been known as Dissenters or Nonconformists and have existed in various forms since the Reformation. In the course of history they have developed their own traditions. They probably reached the peak of their influence in the mid-nineteenth century: the 1851 census revealed that the numbers attending Dissenting services almost equalled the worshippers of the Church of England. This is reflected in the fact that, according to a recent survey, 10 per cent of Free Church buildings date from before 1800 while 49 per cent were built in the nineteenth century.

In Wales the Free Churches, and in particular Calvinistic Methodism, have historically been the dominant form of Christianity: the 1851 census of religion found that over 80 per cent of those at worship in Wales attended a nonconformist chapel.

All the major Free Churches—Methodist, Baptist, United Reformed and the Salvation Army—allow both men and women to become ministers. Eighteen of the Free Churches belong to the *Free Church Federal Council* which has existed in its present form since 1940. The Free Church Federal Council has special responsibility for making representations to Government about legislative matters and providing means for the Free Churches' representation at official functions and on national committees. It is also concerned with social and educational issues, the hospital chaplaincy services and evangelism, and has recently taken on a role co-ordinating the ecumenical representation of the smaller denominations in its membership. The Free Churches have a total membership of nearly one million.

The Methodist Church

The Methodist Church, the largest of the Free Churches with just over 430,000 adult full members and a community of more than 1.3 million, originated in the eighteenth century following the evangelical revival launched by John Wesley (1703–91), his brother Charles (1707–88), and George Whitefield (1714–70). The name is probably derived from the practice of following a specified 'method' of devotional study. John Wesley was an ordained member of the Church of England and throughout his life denied that he wished to form a separate denomination. In 1784 Methodism was given a formal constitution in the Deed of Declaration and the first Methodist ordinations took place. In 1787 Methodist chapels and preachers had to be licensed under the Toleration Act, and the Methodists were thereby legally classified as Dissenters. The full separation of the Methodists from the Church of England took place in 1795, when Methodist preachers began to administer the sacraments, after the death of John Wesley. The new denomination was particularly successful in the newly-industrialised areas where the Church of England was not organised.

The present church is based on a 1932 union of most of the separate Methodist churches which had emerged as a result of divisions in the movement. (These were the Wesleyan Methodist

Church, the Primitive Methodist Church and the United Methodist Church.) Its 3,514 ministers and students for the ministry and 7,207 places of worship are organised into some 700 circuits which are in turn organised into 33 districts. Circuit meetings comprise ministers and lay officers; district synods, held in autumn and spring, consist of all ministers and selected lay people, chaired by a minister appointed by the Methodist Conference, the governing authority. The church is particularly strong in the north and the south-west of England.

The Methodist Churches which did not join the union include the Independent Methodists, members of the Independent Methodist Connexion of Churches (with nearly 3,600 members, 132 ministers and 104 places of worship) which broke away in 1805; and the Wesleyan Reform Union (with 2,933 members, 21 ministers and 127 places of worship) which broke away in 1849. The latter is Methodist in doctrine and congregational (see p. 35) in organisation; its membership is concentrated in Yorkshire. The Methodist Church in Ireland has over 14,000 members in Northern Ireland.

Baptists

The Baptist movement first achieved an organised form in Britain in the seventeenth century: the first church was established in England in 1612. In 1641 the Particular Baptists, who adhered to Calvinist ideas, officially adopted the rite of immersion in water, the practice from which Baptists get their name. Although they benefited from the fact that the government of the Commonwealth under Oliver Cromwell and his son (see p. 18) was relatively tolerant, this period of toleration ended with the restoration of the monarchy of 1660. At this time one of the best-known Baptist leaders, John Bunyan, the author of *The Pilgrim's Progress*, was imprisoned for 12 years.

The Baptists emphasise the interdependency of individual churches, which are mainly organised in groups or associations of churches, most of which belong to the Baptist Union of Great Britain (formed in 1812), with a membership of about 160,000. The Union has about 2,000 ministers and 2,150 places of worship. There are also separate Baptist Unions for Scotland, Wales and Ireland, with some overlap of membership, and other Baptist Churches, including the Old Baptist Union (with about 500 members, 8 ministers and 15 places of worship) and Associations of Strict Baptists. The Baptists are particularly well represented in south-east England and East Anglia. International Baptist bodies include the Baptist World Alliance.

United Reformed Church

The United Reformed Church, with some 118,000 members, 1,016 ministers (both stipendiary and non-stipendiary) and 1,792 places of worship, was formed in 1972, when the Congregational Church in England and Wales and the Presbyterian Church of England merged. This was the first union of two different churches in England since the Reformation in the sixteenth century. In 1981 there was a further union with the *Re-formed Association of the Churches of Christ*.

The *Congregational Church* is the oldest Protestant minority in Britain; its origins can be traced back to the Puritans of sixteenth-century England. The Church's name was derived from the fact that all authority was vested in the congregation. *Presbyterianism* was briefly the national church (1645–60) during the period of the Commonwealth, but owed this somewhat nominal position to the presence of a Scottish army. (The Church of Scotland is to this day Presbyterian—see p. 28.) Relatively few Presbyterian congregations survived beyond the eighteenth century, and the growth of Presbyterianism in the nineteenth century and its survival into the twentieth century were largely due to immigration from Scotland. Scottish influence continues to be reflected in the church's strength in Northumberland and in areas where Scottish immigrants settled. The church is also particularly well represented in East Anglia, reflecting the historic strength of the Congregational chapels in the region.

The United Reformed Church's central body, the General Assembly, consists of equal numbers of ministers and lay members. The church is divided into 12 provinces, each of which has a provincial moderator who chairs the provincial synod; these are further divided into 68 districts.

There is a separate Congregational Federation, which consists of those Congregational churches which did not join the United Reformed Church. It has nearly 10,000 members, 109 ministers and 286 churches. The Fellowship of the Churches of Christ (see below) includes churches which did not take part in the 1981 merger.

The Salvation Army

The Salvation Army was founded in 1865. Formed in the East End of London by William Booth (1829–1912), a former Methodist preacher, it was originally known as the Christian Mission, receiving its present name in 1878. Within Britain there are 55,000 members and nearly 1,000 centres of worship. There are about 1,792 active full-time officers with a quasi-military command structure, headed by a General who is elected by a High

The Remembrance Service in Glasgow Cathedral, following the Gulf War.

The Queen meeting leaders of different religious communities attending the Commonwealth Day service at Westminster Abbey in March 1991 (see p. 67).

Salisbury Cathedral, one of the best known of the Church of England's buildings.

The Right Reverend George Carey at his enthronement as Archbishop of Canterbury in April 1991.

The Church of England General Synod (see p. 21).

The General Secretary and Presidents of the Council of Churches for Britain and Ireland (see p. 67) in front of Liverpool's Roman Catholic Cathedral at the Council's inaugural assembly in 1990.

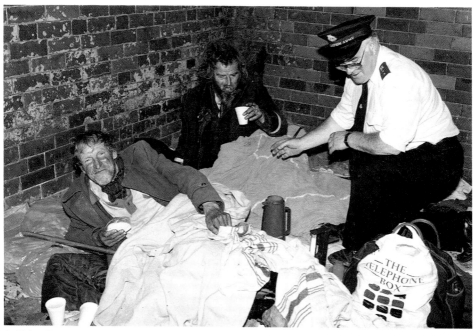

A Salvation Army officer helping homeless people in Glasgow.

A Methodist chapel in Wales.

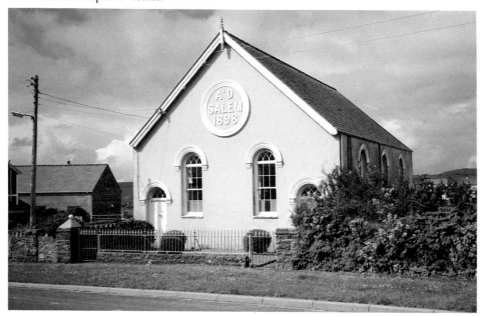

A service in the Celestial Church in Brixton, London.

The Chief Rabbi (in the centre at the back of the picture) attending a special inauguration day.

Muslims worshipping in a mosque in Bradford.

The Central Mosque in London's Regent's Park (see p. 54).

The celebration of a traditional Hindu festival in north London.

The celebration of a Sikh wedding in London.

Buddhists attending an event at the Peace Pagoda in Battersea Park, London.

The Tibetan Buddhist temple of Samye Ling in Dumfriesshire, opened in 1988 (see p. 60).

A detail from the interior of the Jain temple in Leicester (see p. 61).

Council of senior officers. Its quasi-military nature is also reflected in its uniforms and its bands.

The Salvation Army's distinctive ministry of Christian evangelism and practical care is expressed through the work of its 130 social service centres, which range from hostels for the homeless to homes for those in need, and through its prison chaplaincy service, which covers 96 prisons. The Army operates in 93 countries; London serves as its international headquarters.

Other Free Churches

The other members of the Free Church Federal Council are:

The Afro-Westindian United Council of Churches (comprising 30,000 individual members, 350 ministers and 250 places of worship), the *Council of African and Afro-Caribbean Churches UK* (comprising 12,000 individual members, 135 ministers and 65 places of worship) and the *New Testament Church of God* (with 7,500 members, 110 ministers and 105 places of worship). These churches are based among the half-million or so members of the West Indian community in Britain. A recent survey suggested that there were altogether 164 black-led Christian churches in Britain, many of which consisted of individual congregations. The churches are concentrated in the larger urban areas, particularly inner London, and constitute one of the fastest growing Christian groupings in Britain.

The British Province of the Moravian Church has been active in England since the early eighteenth century, receiving legal recognition in 1749. The Moravian Church is a Protestant episcopal church descended from the Bohemian Brethren of the fifteenth century; it was revived after 1722 by Count von Zinzendorf (d. 1760) on his estates in Saxony. The Moravians formerly lived in self-supporting communities but are now chiefly active as an international missionary church. They have had considerable influence over other Christians: those influenced by their thinking have included John Wesley (see p. 33) and the Countess of Huntingdon (see below), while their communities inspired the Christian Socialist movement. They have 2,579 members, 26 ministers and 38 places of worship.

The Countess of Huntingdon's Connexion was founded by Selina, Countess of Huntingdon (1707–91) in 1779. She was formerly a Moravian (see above) and a member of the Wesleys' Methodist Society (see p. 33). The Connexion has 900 members, 14 ministers and 24 places of worship.

The Fellowship of the Churches of Christ (see p. 36) is also known in the United States as the 'Disciples of Christ'. Although their origins can be traced to the eighteenth century they became an organised community in Britain in 1842. They have a congregational system of government and an ordained ministry; there are 1,143 members, 17 ministers and 37 places of worship.

The Free Church of England (or *Reformed Episcopal Church*) was formed in 1844 by James Shore, a Church of England clergyman in the Diocese of Exeter, in direct response to the Oxford Movement (see p. 40). The church was at first Presbyterian and later became episcopal. It has 1,367 members, 30 ministers and 27 places of worship.

The Presbyterian (or *Calvinistic Methodist*) *Church of Wales* arose from a revivalist movement led in 1735 by Howell Harris, a Welsh preacher who himself remained a member of the then established Church in Wales. It has a Presbyterian form of government—its 61,616 members include a large section of the

Welsh speaking population. It has 137 ministers and 1,025 places of worship.

The *Union of Welsh Independents* or *Undeb yr Annibynwyr Cymraeg*, which is entirely Welsh speaking, dates back to 1639, and is Calvinistic in doctrine and congregational in organisation. It has 50,612 members, 126 ministers and 630 places of worship.

Northern Ireland

The Free Churches in Northern Ireland do not belong to the Free Church Federal Council. They include the Presbyterian Church in Ireland, with 350,000 members, 400 ministers and 565 congregations, and the Non-Subscribing Presbyterian Church of Ireland. Many of their members are descended from Scottish Presbyterian settlers.

The Roman Catholic Church

History

The formal structure of the Roman Catholic Church in England and Wales, which ceased to exist after the Reformation in the sixteenth century (see p. 17), was restored in 1850. The Scottish Church's formal structure ceased to exist in the early seventeenth century and was restored in 1878. As a result the overwhelming majority of the Roman Catholic churches in Britain have been built since the mid-nineteenth century: an estimated 62 per cent of those in England have been built this century.

However, throughout this period Catholicism never disappeared entirely, although much of the Catholic population is descended from Irish immigrants who began to arrive in large numbers in the nineteenth century. This is still reflected in the church's strength in the north-west of England, and especially Merseyside; elsewhere Catholicism tends to be stronger in urban rather than rural areas.

There have also been a large number of conversions to Roman Catholicism. The first major development of this kind was in the 1840s, when, influenced by the Oxford or Tractarian Movement, which began as an Anglican revival movement, a number of prominent converts from the Church of England joined the Roman Catholic Church. They included the Anglican clergyman and theologian John Henry Newman, who became a Roman Catholic Cardinal.

Structure

There are now seven Roman Catholic provinces in Great Britain, each under an archbishop, and 30 dioceses, each under a bishop (22 in England and Wales; the two provinces and eight dioceses in Scotland are independently responsible to the Pope). In Northern Ireland there are six dioceses, some with territory partly in the Irish Republic. There is normally one cardinal for Scotland, one for England and one for Ireland (covering both the Irish Republic and Northern Ireland). About 250 Roman Catholic religious orders, congregations and societies are represented in Britain.

The Roman Catholic Church in England and Wales is governed by a Bishops' Conference, whose membership includes diocesan bishops, the Apostolic Exarch of the Ukrainians in Britain, the bishop of the armed forces and auxiliary bishops. The Conference is divided into five departments with different responsibilities. Between conference sessions there is a Bishops' Standing Committee consisting of the archbishops and chairmen of departments. It is serviced by a general secretariat. There are a number of affiliated agencies and consultative bodies.

There is a separate Bishops' Conference in Scotland and an Irish Episcopal Conference which covers the whole of Ireland.

There are over 2,800 parishes. The church has little inherited wealth: the 22 dioceses administer funds on behalf of the parishes. About one British citizen in ten normally claims to be a Roman Catholic. There are 6,200 priests; only men may become priests.

Education

The Roman Catholic Church attaches great importance to the education of its children and requires its members to try to bring up their children in the Catholic faith. There are about 2,500 Catholic schools in Britain. A number of Catholic schools are staffed by members of religious orders (to the extent of one teacher in 20). The orders also undertake other social work. The majority of Catholic schools are maintained out of public funds and new schools may be established with government grants (see p. 9).

Other Congregations

The Roman Catholic Church in Britain also includes separately organised congregations for about 25 different nationalities, including the Chinese, Croatians, Czechs, Filipinos, French, Hungarians, Italians, Lithuanians, Germans, Poles, Spaniards, Vietnamese and West Indians.

Newspapers

Three Catholic newspapers, *The Tablet*, the *Catholic Herald* and *The Universe*, are published weekly.

Relations with the Papacy

In 1982 Pope John Paul II paid a pastoral visit to Britain, the first by a reigning pope. The Pope has been diplomatically represented in Britain by an Apostolic Pro-Nuncio since 1982 (between 1938 and 1982 the Pope was represented by an Apostolic Delegation).

Other Christian Churches and Groups

The Unitarian Churches

The Unitarians, whose origins are traceable to the Reformation, have 10,000 members, 154 ministers and 163 places of worship; their first place of worship was opened in London in 1774 and they were recognised by law in 1813. The Unitarian Churches have no formal creed and do not subscribe to the prevailing Christian doctrine of the Trinity (hence 'Unitarian', a reference to their belief in the unity of God as one person). Unitarian congregations may also include theists and humanists. The Unitarian churches in Britain are organised into the General Assembly of Unitarian and Free Christian Churches, founded in 1928. The Unitarian Churches have traditionally been most strongly represented in the towns and cities of northern England and the Midlands.

Pentecostalist Churches

The Pentecostalist movement began in the early twentieth century following a revival in Los Angeles in 1906; the first revival meetings in Britain took place in 1907. The name 'Pentecostalists' refers to the events of the Pentecost described in the New Testament of the Bible (*Acts of the Apostles*, Chapter 2). Pentecostalist worship can include speaking in tongues and spiritual healing. The two main bodies operating in Britain are the

Assemblies of God and the Elim Pentecostal Church, many
of whose members are of West Indian origin. There are a
total of over 1,000 Pentecostalist churches with about 68,000
members, concentrated in urban areas and particularly inner
London.

The Society of Friends

The Religious Society of Friends, with about 18,000 adult
members in Britain and 450 places of worship, was founded in
the middle of the seventeenth century under the leadership
of George Fox (1624–91); the movement belonged to the
radical wing of the later period of the English Reformation.
They are commonly known as *Quakers*, which may be a reference
to the trembling that allegedly happened among those attending
early meetings. Organisation takes the form of weekly meetings
for worship, monthly meetings and general meetings; elders
and overseers have particular responsibility for the spiritual
and pastoral aspects of Quaker life respectively. The highest
authority is the London Yearly Meeting (which does not necess-
arily meet in London). It appoints a Meeting for Sufferings (the
title is a legacy from the times when the Quakers were persecuted)
which meets about ten times a year and appoints other central
committees. Silent worship is central to the Society's life as a
religious organisation; there is no ordained ministry and there are
no sacraments. The Friends are represented in 40 countries and
work for peace and the relief of suffering in many parts of the
world.

The Friends' School Joint Council co-ordinates the work
of the eight Friends' schools in Britain. The Friends also

run Woodbrooke College, one of the Selly Oak Colleges[1] in Birmingham. It is a centre for religious, social, peace and international studies. There are also a number of study centres, summer schools, homes for the elderly and a psychiatric hospital (which, when it was established in 1796, was the first to be set up in England). The influence of the Quakers on British society has traditionally been greater than their numbers might suggest.

Quaker publications include a weekly, *The Friend*, *The Friends' Quarterly*, *Quaker Monthly* and *The Young Quaker*. The Friends' Library in London has 60,000 books and pamphlets and 50,000 manuscripts.

The House Church Movement or New Churches

A recent development in Christian worship has been the 'house church movement', which began in the early 1970s and now has an estimated membership of almost 110,000, largely made up of former members of Protestant denominations. Originally members held services in private houses, taking turns to chair meetings. However most groups have now outgrown private houses and use a variety of hired buildings. These non-denominational congregations may come together as 'streams', of which some of the better-known are New Frontiers, Pioneer and *Ichthus*. The churches receive money from their members to enable them to support their leaders and carry out missionary and social work.

---

[1]A private institution involved in adult education and training in social work, education, peace studies, Christianity and interfaith dialogue; the colleges are affiliated to Birmingham University.

Christian Brethren

The Christian Brethren are a Protestant body influenced by Calvinism; they were organised in their present form by J. N. Darby (1800–82), formerly a Church of Ireland minister. There are no ordained clergy. The first congregation was established in 1831 in Plymouth, giving rise to the name 'Plymouth Brethren', a title the Brethren reject. They remain relatively well represented in south-west England. The Brethren are divided into two branches, the Open Brethren (with an estimated 43,500 members) and the Closed or Exclusive Brethren (with an estimated 7,600 members).

Church of the New Jerusalem or New Church (Swedenborgians)

The Church of the New Jerusalem, a small non-Trinitarian group, was first organised in Britain in 1787 to follow the teachings of Emanuel Swedenborg (1688–1772), a Swedish scientist, philosopher and theologian who died in England.

Christadelphians

The Christadelphians are a small anti-Trinitarian sect organised into individual *'ecclesias'* or congregations. They were founded by John Thomas (1805–71), an English doctor who emigrated to the United States.

Overseas Churches Represented in Britain

A number of Christian communities of foreign origin have established their own centres of worship, especially during the twentieth century and particularly in London.

Orthodox Churches

A large number of Orthodox churches from different countries are represented in Britain, with an estimated total of about 270,000 members. There are about 200 places of worship and a similar number of priests. The first Orthodox church was a Greek Orthodox Church established in Greek Street, London, in 1677. The present Greek Cathedral in Bayswater, London, dates from 1879. Larger numbers of Orthodox Christians arrived in Britain from Greece after the outbreak of the Greek war of independence in 1821 and from Russia after the Russian revolution of 1917. More Orthodox Christians arrived from Eastern Europe after the second world war, and many more Greek Orthodox Christians arrived from Cyprus.

The Orthodox churches in Britain include the Greek Orthodox (the Ecumenical Patriarchate), and those of Russia (the Moscow Patriarchate and the Russian Orthodox Church Outside Russia), Serbia and Romania; and the Ukrainian Autocephalous Orthodox Church and the Byelorussian Autocephalous Orthodox Church. The Orthodox Patriarchate of Antioch has one priest in Britain. The Coptic Orthodox Church is represented in London.

Other eastern Christian groups represented in London include the Armenian Church and the Assyrian Church of the East.

Lutheran Churches

There are about 100 Lutheran churches in Britain (churches inspired by the teaching of the German Protestant reformer Martin Luther—1483–1546). These include congregations for people from the Scandinavian and Baltic countries and for Hungarian and Polish Lutherans. Most belong to the Lutheran Council of Great Britain. There are also Lutheran churches established as a result

of American mission activity in Britain; these comprise the
Evangelical Lutheran Church of England.

Other Churches

The Reformed Protestant Churches of various European countries
are represented in Britain; there are, for example, French and
Swiss Protestant churches in London. There are also Chinese and
American churches in London.

All these churches operate in a variety of languages.

Other Organisations

There are also several other religious organisations in Britain
which were founded in the United States in the last century.
These include:

—the Jehovah's Witnesses, founded by C.T. Russell (1852–1916),
with an estimated 120,000 adult members in Britain who gather
in an estimated 1,300 'kingdom halls';

—the Church of Jesus Christ of the Latter-Day Saints (the
Mormon Church), founded by Joseph Smith (1805–44) who was
succeeded by Brigham Young (1801–77), with an estimated
150,000 members, about 400 places of worship and almost
10,000 ministers in Britain;

—the Christian Scientists or the Churches of Christ Scientist,
founded by Mary Baker Eddy (1821–1910) and based on the idea
of spiritual healing. They do not publish statistics but have some
215 branch churches in Britain;

—the Seventh-Day Adventists, founded by William Miller (d. 1849); and

—the Spiritualists, arising in their present form from the experiences of the American Fox family in 1848, with an estimated 60,000 adult members in Britain and about 600 buildings.

Other Religions

The Jewish Community

History

Although Jews were probably present in Britain in Roman times, they were first recorded as settling in England at the time of the Norman Conquest in the latter half of the eleventh century; by the twelfth century there were Jewish communities in most of the large cities. However, the entire community was expelled in 1290. The present community in Britain dates from 1656, when Jews were readmitted; it was founded by Jews of Spanish and Portuguese origin (known as Sephardim). Larger numbers of Jews came to Britain from Eastern Europe in the late nineteenth and early twentieth centuries, and in the 1930s large numbers arrived from Germany and Central Europe. Jews from Eastern and Central Europe are known as Ashkenazim.

Structure

The present Jewish community, numbering about 300,000, is the second largest in Europe (after that in France and in the countries of the former Soviet Union). About two-thirds of the community, totalling about 200,000, live in London. There is a community of about 27,000 in Manchester and there are other sizeable communities in Leeds, Glasgow and Brighton.

The community is divided into two main groups. Some 77 per cent of the majority Ashkenazi Jews are *Orthodox* and most acknowledge the authority of the Chief Rabbi. The Chief Rabbi is appointed by the United Synagogue, founded in 1870, the main religious body of Orthodox Jewry in Britain. The Sephardi Orthodox element follow their own spiritual head (the Haham); they are organised into the Spanish and Portuguese Jews' Congregation, founded in 1657. The *Reform Movement*, founded in 1840, the *Liberal and Progressive Movement*, established in 1901, and the recently established *Masorti Movement* account for most of the remaining 23 per cent of British Jews; their organisations include the Reform Synagogues of Great Britain, the Union of Liberal and Progressive Synagogues and the Assembly of Masorti Synagogues.

There are about 356 Jewish congregations in Britain. Synagogue services are held on Saturdays as part of the celebration of the Jewish Sabbath. The Jewish Bible or Tenakh comprises the Law books (or Torah), the Prophets (or Nevi'im), and the Writings (or Ketubim).

Education

About one in three Jewish children attend Jewish schools (some of them supported by public funds). There are altogether 36 primary schools and 17 secondary schools as well as two public schools offering boarding facilities. The Jews' College, founded in 1855, which confers London University degrees, provides education for intending rabbis. There are separate colleges for training Reform and Liberal and Sephardic rabbis. There are a number of agencies, including the Jewish Welfare Board, which care for elderly and handicapped people.

The Board of Deputies

The officially recognised representative body is the *Board of Deputies of British Jews*, established in 1760. It has the right to petition the Crown and the deputies are consulted on relevant legislation. The Board consists of over 600 deputies, mainly elected by synagogues. It belongs to the World Jewish Congress.

Newspapers and Broadcasting

A national newspaper, the *Jewish Chronicle*, founded in 1841, is published weekly. Its subsidiaries include the *Leeds Jewish Gazette* and the *Manchester Jewish Gazette*. The *Jewish Chronicle* also publishes the *Jewish Yearbook*. LBC radio in London broadcasts a half-hour programme *You Don't Have to be Jewish* each week and there are programmes for the Jewish community on other local radio stations.

The Muslim Community

History

The religion of Islam (the word means 'submission'—to God) originated in Makkah (now in Saudi Arabia) in the seventh century AD. The Prophet Muhammad, who Muslims believe was the messenger who communicated the religion to mankind, was born in AD 570 in Makkah and died in 632. Today there are well over 1,000 million Muslims in the world, inhabiting most of the countries between Morocco and south-east Asia. In addition to all the states of North Africa and the Middle East where the Arabic language is spoken, Turkey, Iran, Afghanistan, Pakistan, Bangladesh and Malaysia are Muslim countries. There are also large Muslim populations in Africa south of the Sahara and in some of the southern republics of the former Soviet Union, the People's Republic of China, India, Indonesia and the Philippines. Britain's close links with the Muslim world can be traced back over many centuries, and arose both from Britain's position as a major trading nation and as an imperial power. Early British converts to Islam included William Quillian, who founded an Islamic Institute and a mosque in Liverpool; and Lord Headley, who announced his conversion in 1913 and helped found the British Muslim Association.

Population

The most recent estimates suggest that Britain's Muslim population is around one million, making it the largest non-Christian community in the country. The largest number originate from Pakistan and Bangladesh (in 1986 there were about 430,000 people of Pakistani origin and 108,000 people of Bangladeshi origin in Britain), while sizeable groups have come from India, Cyprus, the Arab world, Malaysia and parts of Africa. There is also a growing community of British-born Muslims, mainly the children of immigrant parents, but including an increasing number of converts to Islam from among the existing population. The latter are estimated to number about 30,000.

Mosques

There are some 600 mosques and numerous prayer centres throughout Britain: 35 years ago there were fewer than ten. About 30 of the mosques are purpose-built. Mosques are not only places of worship; they also offer instruction in the Muslim way of life and facilities for educational and welfare activities. The first was established at Woking in Surrey in 1890, and they now range from converted houses in many industrial towns to the Central Mosque in London and its associated Islamic Cultural Centre, one of the most important Muslim institutions in the Western world. Opened in 1976, the Central Mosque has the largest congregation in Britain, which during festivals may number over 5,000. The trustees of the Centre are the heads of mission of the Muslim governments represented in London. There are also important mosques and cultural centres in Liverpool, Manchester, Leicester, Bradford, Edinburgh and Glasgow.

Many of the mosques belong to various Muslim organisations. Both the Sunni and the Shia traditions within Islam are represented among the Muslim community in Britain, as is the Ismaili sect whose international leader is the Aga Khan. Members of some of the major Sufi traditions have also developed branches in British cities.

Muslim Organisations

The Muslim community in Britain has formed a very large number of national and local organisations. Most are concerned with religious, educational, social and welfare activities; some have been established for the benefit of a particular national group; and others for the members of a particular profession. Among the more active are the *Muslim World League*, an international organisation which opened its London office in 1984, and the *Union of Muslim Organisations of the United Kingdom and Eire*, a co-ordinating body which was formed in 1970 and has over 180 Muslim organisations affiliated to it.

Education

In 1978 the National Muslim Education Council of the United Kingdom was established to co-ordinate all Islamic educational activities in Britain and to establish Muslim single-sex schools in areas with large Muslim communities. The establishment of an Islamic University in Britain is a longer-term aim. The Muslim World League sponsors professors at Cambridge and London universities and is also involved in issues relating to education in schools. There are a number of Muslim-run schools and colleges which train *imams* for mosques in Britain.

Islamic Studies

British contacts with the Islamic world date back to medieval times, when English scholars visited Spain, then a centre of Islamic culture under Moorish rule. In 1632 the first British chair of Arabic was founded at Cambridge, followed four years later by a similar professorship at Oxford. During the eighteenth century, knowledge of Islamic studies became more widespread and one of the first English translations of the Qur'an was made. In the nineteenth century travel to the Islamic world became increasingly common and a number of important works were translated from numerous languages used in Islamic countries.

In the twentieth century there has been a deliberate policy to expand the range of facilities in British universities for the study of all aspects of Islamic civilisation. One of the most important centres is the School of Oriental and African Studies, established in 1916 by the University of London. The universities of Oxford, Cambridge, Durham and St Andrews also have departments of Middle Eastern and Islamic Studies; many other universities teach related subjects.

The Sikh Community

History

The Sikh religion stems from the teaching of the ten Sikh Gurus who were active in northern India for over two centuries: the word Sikh means 'learner'. The first Guru, Guru Nanak, lived from 1469 to 1539. The last Guru, Guru Gobind Singh, died in 1708. Guru Gobind Singh established the five 'K's (the letter 'k' is taken from the Punjabi initials of the words) which all Sikhs are required to observe: uncut hair (*kes*); wearing a comb to keep the hair tidy (*khangha*); wearing a wrist band on the right arm (*kara*); wearing a sword or dagger (*kirpan*); and wearing trousers (*kachh*). Sikhs are exempted from the British legal requirement to wear crash helmets when riding motor cycles provided they wear turbans. Men's names are followed by the word '*Singh*' meaning lion, and women's names by word '*Kaur*' meaning princess. The Sikh scriptures are called the *Guru Granth Sahib*.

Population

There is a large Sikh community in Britain, comprising over 300,000, the members of which originate mainly from India. Most came from the Punjab in north-west India, although a large minority have come via East Africa (in 1986–88 there were an estimated 800,000 people in Britain—of all religions—who were by origin from India). The largest groups of Sikhs are in Greater London, Manchester, Birmingham, Nottingham and Wolverhampton. There are also a number of Sikh sectarian groups; some—Namdharis and Nirankaris—stress the importance of living gurus, in addition to the ten Gurus mentioned above.

Gurdwaras

Sikh temples or *gurdwaras* cater for the religious, educational, social welfare, and cultural needs of their community. Most Sikhs attend their *gurdwara* each Sunday for a regular service, although worship may take place on other days; special services are held at the time of Sikh festivals (see p. 72). The oldest central *gurdwara* in London was established in 1908 and the largest is in Southall, Middlesex. There are over 160 *gurdwaras* in Britain. *Gurdwaras* are generally managed by committees, elected by regular congregations. A *granthi* is normally employed to take care of the building and to conduct the prayers.

Sikh Organisations and Publications

One of the main Sikh organisations in Britain, the Sikh Missionary Society, was founded in 1969 in Gravesend. It is now based in Southall, London. The Sikh Cultural Society of Great Britain was established in 1960.

The *Sikh Courier International*, founded in 1960, and the *Sikh Messenger*, founded in 1984, are published in Britain on a quarterly basis.

The Hindu Community

History

The Hindu religion has developed over at least 4,000 years in the South Asian sub-continent; the words 'Hindu' and 'India' are by origin linked. The Hindu scriptures comprise a range of ancient writings including the four *Vedas*, the *Upanishads*, the epics the *Mahabharata* and the *Ramayana*, the *Laws of Manu* and the *Puranas*. The *Mahabharata* includes the *Bhagavad Gita*.

Population

The Hindu community in Britain comprises around 300,000 members originating largely from India. It is one of the most recent of the south Asian communities to develop in Britain: although some Hindus arrived directly from India in the 1950s and the early 1960s, most, although of Indian origin, came from East Africa in the late 1960s and early 1970s. Some, again of Indian origin, have come from other parts of the world, including Fiji and Trinidad. Many Hindus in Britain—about 40 per cent—are originally from the Indian province of Gujarat; the other large group—about 35 per cent—come originally from the Punjab. The largest groups of Hindus are to be found in different areas of London, Birmingham, Bradford and Leicester.

Worship

Hindu families generally have an area for worship in their own homes, which includes pictures and often statues of particular deities, such as Krishna, Rama, Ganesh and Ambamata or Durgmata and sometimes gurus, such as Satya Sai Baba, and Pramukh Swami. Hindus are not required to attend a place of worship regularly, but large numbers attend Hindu temples for the annual festivals (see p. 71). The first Hindu temple or *mandir* was opened in London in 1962; there are now over 150 *mandirs* in Britain. Some *mandirs* represent mainstream Hindu practice, while others belong to different organisations such as the Satya Sai Baba Fellowship or the International Society for Krishna Consciousness (see p. 63). A number are affiliated to the National Council of Hindu Temples, and to the Vishwa Hindu Parishad, an international Hindu organisation. The varieties of practice among Hindus in Britain reflect both the diversity within

Hinduism and the fact that the community comes from a range of areas, backgrounds and traditions.

Buddhism

History

Buddhism is a modern Western term used to refer to a wide range of mental and spiritual cultures, all developed from the teaching of Siddhartha Gautama the Buddha, who lived and taught in north-east India in the sixth century BC. His teachings are set out in the *Tripitaka*, although the different schools of Buddhism have developed and use other versions of the texts. All the main schools of Buddhism are represented in Britain today. They include Theravada, the prevailing school in Sri Lanka, Thailand and Burma; Zen, found in Japan and China; and Tibetan Buddhism.

The origins of British interest in Buddhism can be traced back to the collection and translation of Buddhist texts, a substantial number of which were published in the late nineteenth and early twentieth centuries: in 1881 the Pali Text Society, which has been responsible for the publication of many of the main Buddhist texts, was formed. At the same time many Britons serving in British colonies in the Far East experienced Buddhism at first hand; a number were among the early translators of Buddhist works.

In 1907 the Buddhist Society of Great Britain and Ireland was established. It was the forerunner of the present Buddhist Society, whose origins go back to 1924, when it was founded as a lodge of the Theosophical Society (see p. 63). The founder President of the Buddhist Society, Christmas Humphreys (1901–83), who was also a distinguished lawyer and judge, was for many years the most prominent figure in British Buddhism and wrote numerous books on the subject.

The first school of Buddhism established in Britain—in the late nineteenth and early twentieth centuries—was the Theravada. This was in large part due to Britain's colonial ties with Sri Lanka (then known as Ceylon). Subsequently an increasing number of translations of Zen Buddhist works appeared. The Tibetan school received its main impetus from the events following the Chinese occupation of Tibet in 1959: as a result a number of senior Tibetan lamas (or monks) settled in Britain.

Wider opportunities for travel in the 1960s led to many young people from Britain travelling to the Far East and encountering Buddhist communities; this coincided with a general interest in new spiritual approaches and has contributed to the fact that the Buddhist community in Britain largely consists of adherents of British or Western origin, although there are small numbers of Buddhists from Vietnam, Japan, Tibet, Thailand and Sri Lanka. Buddhist thought has also had a considerable influence over a number of new religious movements and the New Age movement.

Buddhist Groups

There are about 150 Buddhist groups and some 50 centres in Britain, with at least 20 monasteries (or *sanghas*) and a number of temples. The Tibetan Buddhist Temple of Samye Ling, in Dumfriesshire, Scotland, which opened in 1988, has been described as the largest and most splendid of its kind in the Western world (see illustration section). To a lesser degree, the same applies to the Thai Buddhapadipa Temple (founded in 1966) in Wimbledon, London, where a traditional, richly decorated shrine room and ceremonial hall were opened in 1982. There are also two peace pagodas, at Milton Keynes, in Buckinghamshire, and in Battersea Park, London.

The Buddhist Society, with its headquarters in London, promotes the principles of Buddhism; it does not belong to any particular school of Buddhism. Its quarterly journal, *The Middle Way*, is believed to be the most widely circulated Buddhist periodical in the West; it also publishes *The Buddhist Directory*, which gives details of Buddhist Societies and organisations in Britain and elsewhere. The Society runs a programme of lectures and classes as well as a correspondence course and a summer school.

Other Religious Groups

Jainism
There are about 30,000 Jains in Britain, mainly living in London, Leicester and Coventry. The Jain or Jaina religion is of ancient Indian origin: the name is derived from the ancient *'jinas'*—'those who overcome'; Jain tradition refers to 24 such figures. The community in Britain is by origin from India (today most Jains live in Gujarat and Rajastan in western India), although most have come from East Africa. A Jain temple (or *derasar*) was opened in Leicester in 1988 (see illustration section).

Zoroastrianism
The Zoroastrian religion (or Mazdaism) originated in ancient Iran. The name is derived from a European version (Zoroaster) of Zarathushtra, the person who is believed to have founded the

religion and who is often dated to around 1000 BC. The term 'Mazdaism' is derived from 'Ahura Mazda', the 'Wise Lord'.

The Parsi community, which comprises Zoroastrians who are by origin from the South Asian sub-continent, has links with Britain going back over 200 years; it has the longest history of settlement of all the South Asian groups in Britain. In some cases Zoroastrians in Britain have come from the sub-continent via East Africa; others have come from Iran. There are an estimated 5,000 Zoroastrians in Britain. Festivals and life-cycle rites are conducted at a centre in London. The World Zoroastrian Organisation was set up in London in 1980.

The Baha'i Community

The Baha'i movement originated in nineteenth-century Iran, deriving its name from its founder Baha'ullah (1817–92). It regards all the major religions as divine in origin and considers that although each religion has had its own special historical context, each has contributed to a process of progress towards world harmony. In keeping with this the Baha'is support many institutions dedicated to world affairs. There are an estimated 5,000 Baha'is in Britain, organised into 500 local assemblies, administered by the National Spiritual Assembly in London.

New Religious Movements and the role of INFORM

A large number of new religious movements or cults, mostly established since the second world war, and often with overseas origins, are active in Britain. Many incorporate ideas from the major world religions; Eastern religions such as Hinduism and Buddhism have been particularly influential. The interest in such movements was foreshadowed by a growing interest during the late nineteenth and early twentieth centuries in alternative religious philosophies.

This interest found expression through a number of groups. These included the Theosophical Society, which was founded in New York in 1875 by the Russian clairvoyante Helene Blavatsky (1831–91); its leadership in the twentieth century passed for a time to Annie Besant, the social reformer. The society's headquarters are in India. Other groups included the Anthroposophical Society of Rudolf Steiner (1861–1925), an Austrian; and the Gurdjieff Society and related groups which were inspired by Georgei Ivanovitch Gurdjieff (1874–1949), who was born in a part of Armenia which then belonged to the Russian Empire (he later established a centre in France). These groups, which remain active today, stimulated interest in oriental religion.

It has been estimated that today about 500 new religious movements are active in Britain, although there are no clear criteria for what constitutes a new religious movement. It has also been estimated that, while hundreds of thousands of people may have had some contact with a movement, there have been no more than 15,000 committed members of movements at any one time. Some examples of the better-known movements are given below.

Hare Krishna Movement
The Hare Krishna movement has links with the Hindu religious tradition. The International Society for Krishna Consciousness (ISKCON) was founded in 1966 by A. C. Bhaktivedanta Swami Prahupada, who travelled to the United States from India. His disciples became active in Britain in 1968 and established a temple in 1969. They are perhaps best known for their frequent

processions through the streets of large towns and cities during which members, often wearing orange robes, chant and strike tambourines. The organisation has 15 centres in Britain.

Rajneeshism

Rajneeshism takes its name from the Bhagwan Shree Rajneesh (1931–90), an Indian, who established meditation centres in a number of countries where people engaged in a wide variety of activities. In the early 1980s many thousands of people were involved and it was perhaps the fastest growing alternative religious movement. The Bhagwan later returned to Poona in India from the United States, and was latterly known as Osho Rajneesh.

Rastafarianism

Rastafarianism grew out of the 'Back to Africa' movement founded by Marcus Garvey (1887–1940), who was born in Jamaica; in its present form it includes a range of ideas and there are a number of Rastafarian organisations. It takes its name from Ras Tafari, Emperor Haile Selassie of Ethiopia (1892–1975), who was crowned in 1930. Rastafarianism has attracted support among the black population in Britain since the 1950s.

Church of Scientology

The Church of Scientology was founded in 1954 by an American, L. Ron Hubbard (1911–86), author of *Dianetics: The Modern Science of Mental Health*. This described a set of psychotherapeutic exercises concerned with the nature and perfectibility of the mind.

Transcendental Meditation

The Transcendental Meditation (TM) movement was founded by an Indian, Maharishi Mahesh Yogi (1911–), who introduced his ideas to the West in 1958. TM involves a technique which requires study; individuals pay for tuition. The Maharishi International University has been established in the United States.

Unification Church

The Unification Church was founded in the 1950s by a Korean, Sun Myung Moon (1920–)—hence the popular name 'Moonies'. His teachings are set out in the *Divine Principle*. The organisation has an estimated 200 full-time members in Britain.

New Age Movement

The term 'New Age' is commonly used to refer to groups and individuals who share a desire to seek new ideas and experiences of a spiritual or philosophical nature. There is no central organisation, but there are a number of meeting places, guide books and resource centres which offer a wide range of periodicals and other goods and services. The movement is associated with alternative medicine, and ecological issues are also stressed. Some 'New Agers' live in communities. The movement is loosely knit and without any formal leadership; it is thus distinct from the other new religious movements or cults.

New Age ideas may incorporate elements from Christian beliefs, Buddhism, ancient shamanistic and pagan beliefs, witchcraft (or Wicca) and Spiritualism.

INFORM

In response to public concern about the activities of some of the new religious movements, the Government has since 1987 provided funding for the Information Network Focus on Religious Movements (INFORM), an incorporated charity linked to the London School of Economics, which is also supported by the main churches. INFORM is non-political and non-sectarian and does not enter into any debate about particular theological or philosophical positions. Its aims are to conduct research into new religious movements and to provide objective information about them. Those who contact INFORM for help include the relations and friends of people who have become involved in one or other of the movements. INFORM does not offer a counselling service, although it can offer information on, and refer people to, such services; it also organises seminars for counsellors, clergy, social workers and others.

Co-operation between Religions

A number of organisations exist which seek to develop relations between different religions in Britain. They include the *Inter-Faith Network for the United Kingdom*, which links a wide range of organisations with an interest in interfaith relations including representative bodies from the Baha'i, Buddhist, Christian, Hindu, Jain, Jewish, Muslim and Sikh faith communities. Other organisations include the *Council of Christians and Jews*, which works for better understanding among members of the two religions and deals with problems in the social field.

Religious leaders belonging to different faiths have also officiated jointly at a number of important public occasions. Christians, Muslims, Sikhs, Hindus, Jews and Buddhists, for example, have taken part together in the annual religious observance to mark Commonwealth Day, which has been attended by the Queen.

Similar joint events take place when civic services are held in multi-faith towns and cities.

Co-operation among the Churches

The Council of Churches for Britain and Ireland was established in 1990, replacing the former British Council of Churches and taking over its role as the main overall body for the Christian churches in Britain to promote church unity and ecumenical co-operation. Its Assembly meets every two years; church representatives meet twice a year. The Council co-ordinates the work of its 30 member churches who are also grouped in separate ecumenical bodies for England, Scotland, Wales and Ireland: the organisations are called Churches Together in England, Churches Together in Wales (CYTUN), Action of Churches Together in Scotland (ACTS) and the Irish Council of Churches.

The Free Church Federal Council (see p. 32) includes most of the Free Churches of England and Wales. It promotes co-operation among the Free Churches, co-ordinates the ecumenical representation of its smaller denominations and is a channel for communication with government.

Inter-church discussions about the issues involved in the search for unity now take place through international as well as national bodies. The Roman Catholic, Orthodox and Lutheran Churches are represented on some of these as well as the Anglican and some of the Free Churches.

The Anglican Church, the Church of Scotland and the main Free Churches are also members of the *World Council of Churches* (since 1960 the Roman Catholic Church has sent official observers to the Council's main meetings). The Council's origins are usually traced back to the inter-denominational Edinburgh (Missionary) Conference of 1910 which was followed by the Faith and Order Conference in Lausanne in 1927. The present Council was set up in 1948 and held its seventh assembly at Canberra, Australia in 1991. It links together over 300 churches in over 100 countries for co-operation and the study of common problems.

The Sharing of Church Buildings Act 1969 enables agreements to be made by two or more churches for sharing church buildings. A major example of this is in Milton Keynes, where there are 29 united congregations, and the Church of England, Roman Catholics, Baptists, United Reformed Church and Methodists share the new central church under an inter-denominational leader.

Appendix I:
Major Religious Festivals

The names and approximate dates of some of the major festivals celebrated by the different religious groups in Britain are given below. Many groups also celebrate a variety of other festivals. In addition different calendars are used by a number of religious groups and in some cases there may be differences within individual religious groups over the celebration of festivals. The use of a variety of languages means that the names of the festivals can vary.

Buddhism
Buddhist festivals vary from country to country, and between the different schools of Buddhism. The most important ones usually celebrate the major events of the Buddha's life. For the most part they fall on days in the local lunar calendar. There have been moves to establish a general celebration of Buddha Day (or *Wesak*) in May.

Christianity

Festival	*Approximate date*
Christmas (preceded by Advent)	25 December, or 7 January for some Orthodox churches
Easter (preceded by Lent)	March/April

Ascension Day	Thursday after fourth Sunday after Easter
Pentecost or Whit Sunday (also Trinity Sunday for Orthodox Churches)	Seven Sundays after Easter
Trinity Sunday	Sunday after Whit Sunday

Hinduism

A number of religious calendars are in use. Most are lunar. Some of the main festivals are:

Festival	Approximate date
Nava Varsha (New Year)	Around March
Ram Navami (Birthday of Rama, on the ninth day of a specific month)	Around March/April
Raksha Bandan (Festival of Sacred Thread)	Around August
Krishna Janamashtami (Birthday of Krishna)	Around July/August
Navaratri (Nine Nights, worship of Durga, the divine symbol of motherhood)	
Dussehra *or* Vijaya Dashami	Around September–October
Diwali ('Festival of Lights')	September/October
Mahashivatri (worship of Shiva)	January/March
Holi ('Festival of Colours')	February/March

Islam

The Muslim Calendar is calculated in lunar months and thus the years are shorter than years according to the Gregorian calendar. Dates are subject to the visibility of the new moon. Major events include Ramadan (a month of fasting), Id al Fitr (which marks the end of Ramadan), and Id al Adha (the high point of the Hajj or pilgrimage to Makkah and the Holy Places). Some Muslims also celebrate the birthday of Muhammad.

Judaism
Jewish festivals follow a lunar calendar.

Festival	*Approximate date*
Rosh Hashanah (New Year)	September/October
Yom Kippur (Day of Atonement)	September/October
Succoth (Tabernacles)	September/October
Hanukkah	November/December
Purim	February/March
Pesach (Passover)	March/April
Shavuot (Pentecost)	May/June

Sikhism
Sikh festivals follow a lunar calendar.

Festival	*Approximate date*
Baisakhi mela (birthday of the Khalsa or pure ones)	April
Martyrdom of Guru Arjan	May/June
Diwali Mela	October/November
Birth of Guru Nanak	October/November
Martyrdom of Guru Tegh Bahadur	December
Birth of Guru Gobind Singh	December/January
Hola Mohalla Mela	February/March

Appendix II:
Archbishops of Canterbury

For information on the office of Archbishop of Canterbury, see pages 18–21.

597	Augustine	959	Æfsige
604	Laurentius	959	Beorhthelm
619	Mellitus	960	Dunstan
624	Justus	c988	Athelgar
627	Honorius	990	Sigeric Serio
655	Deusdedit	995	Ælfric
668	Theodore	1005	Ælfheah
693	Beorhtweald	1013	Lyfing
731	Tatwine	1020	Æthelnoth
735	Nothelm	1038	Eadsige
740	Cuthbeorht	1051	Robert of Jumièges
761	Breguwine	1052	Stigand
765	Jaenbeorht	1070	Lanfranc
793	Æthelheard	1093	Anselm
805	Wulfred	1114	Ralph d'Escures
832	Feologild	1123	William de Corbeil
833	Ceolnoth	1139	Theobald
870	Æthelred	1162	Thomas Becket
890	Plegmund	1174	Richard [of Dover]
914	Æthelhelm	1185	Baldwin
923	Wulfhelm	1193	Hubert Walter
942	Oda	1207	Stephen Langton

1229	Richard le Grant	1611	George Abbot
1234	Edmund Rich	1633	William Laud
1245	Boniface of Savoy	1660	William Juxon
1273	Robert Kilwardby	1663	Gilbert Sheldon
1279	John Pecham	1678	William Sancroft
1294	Robert Winchelsey	1691	John Tillotson
1313	Walter Reynolds	1695	Thomas Tenison
1328	Simon Mepeham	1716	William Wake
1333	John Stratford	1737	John Potter
1349	Thomas Bradwardine	1747	Thomas Herring
1349	Simon Islip	1757	Matthew Hutton
1366	Simon Langham	1758	Thomas Secker
1368	William Whittlesey	1768	Frederick Cornwallis
1375	Simon Sudbury	1783	John Moore
1381	William Courtenay	1805	Charles Manners Sutton
1396	Thomas Arundel[3]	1828	William Howley
1398	Roger Walden	1848	John Bird Sumner
1414	Henry Chichele	1862	Charles Thomas Longley
1443	John Stafford	1868	Archibald Campbell Tait
1452	John Kemp	1883	Edward White Benson
1454	Thomas Bourchier	1896	Frederick Temple
1486	John Morton	1903	Randall Thomas Davidson
1501	Henry Dean	1928	Cosmo Gordon Lang
1503	William Warham	1942	William Temple
1533	Thomas Cranmer	1945	Geoffrey Francis Fisher
1556	Reginald Pole	1961	Arthur Michael Ramsey
1559	Matthew Parker	1974	Frederick Donald Coggan
1576	Edmund Grindal	1980	Robert Alexander Kennedy Runcie
1583	John Whitgift	1991	George Carey
1604	Richard Bancroft		

[3]Reinstated in 1399.

Addresses

Religious Organisations

Baptist Union of Great Britain
PO Box 44
129 Broadway
Didcot
Oxon OX11 8RT

Buddhist Society
58 Eccleston Square
London SW1V 1PH

Catholic Truth Society
PO Box 422
38–40 Eccleston Square
London SW1V 1PD

General Synod of Church of England
Church House
Great Smith Street
London SW1P 3NZ

Council of Churches for Britain and Ireland
Inter-Church House
35–41 Lower Marsh
London SE1 4RL

Free Church Federal Council
27 Tavistock Square
London WC1H 9HH

Hindu Centre
39 Grafton Terrace
London NW5 4JA

Inter-Faith Network for the United Kingdom
5–7 Tavistock Place
London WC1H 9SS

Islamic Cultural Centre
London Central Mosque
146 Park Road
London NW8 7RG

Methodist Church
1 Central Buildings
London SW1H 9NU

Quaker Information Service
Friends Home Service Committee
Friends House
Euston Road
London NW1 2BJ

Office of the Chief Rabbi
Adler House
Tavistock Square
London WC1H 9HN

Salvation Army
101 Queen Victoria Street
London EC4P 4EP

Church of Scotland
Church Office
121 George Street
Edinburgh EH2 4YN

Sikh Cultural Society of Great Britain
88 Mollison Way
Edgware
Middlesex HA8 5QW

General Assembly of Unitarian and Free Christian Churches
Essex Hall
1–6 Essex Street
London WC2R 3HY

United Reformed Church
86 Tavistock Place
London WC1H 9RT

Government Departments

Department for Education
Sanctuary Buildings
Great Smith Street
London SW1P 3BT

Department of Employment
Caxton House
Tothill Street
London SW1H 9NF

Department of the Environment
2 Marsham Street
London SW1P 3EB

Home Office
Queen Anne's Gate
London SW1H 9AT

Northern Ireland Office
Stormont Castle
Belfast BT4 3ST

Scottish Office
St Andrew's House
Edinburgh EH1 3DE

Welsh Office
Cathays Park
Cardiff CF1 3NQ

Other Organisations

Independent Television Commission
70 Brompton Road
London SW3 1EX

INFORM (Information Network Focus on Religious Movements)
Houghton Street
London WC2A 2AE

Radio Authority
Holbrook House
14 Great Queen Street
London WC2B 5DG

Further Reading

£

BARKER, EILEEN
New Religious Movements. A Practical Introduction.
ISBN 0 11 340927 3.   HMSO   1989   11.95

BRIERLEY, PETER
'Christian' England. What the English Church
Census Reveals. ISBN 1 85321 100 1.   Marc Europe   1991   10.99

HINNELS, JOHN R. (ed.)
Penguin Dictionary of Religions.
ISBN 0 14 051106 7.   Penguin   1984   7.99

Law, Blasphemy and the Multi-Faith Society.
ISBN 1 85442 030 5. Commission for Racial Equality   1990   1.50

SUTHERLAND, STEWART; HOULDEN,
LESLIE; CLARKE, PETER; and HARDY,
FRIEDHELM (eds.) *The World's Religions.*
ISBN 0 415 00324 5.   Routledge   1988   85.00

THOMAS, TERENCE (ed.)
The British. Their Religious Beliefs and
Practices 1800–1986.
ISBN 0 415 01300 3. Paperback.   Routledge   1988   11.99

Directories and Yearbooks

The Buddhist Directory.	Buddhist Society	
The Church of England Year Book.	Church House Publishing	Annual
Crockford's Clerical Directory.	Church House Publishing	Biennial
The Church of Scotland Year Book.	Church of Scotland	Annual
Minutes of Conference and Directory.	Methodist Publishing House	Annual
The Baptist Union Directory.	Baptist Union of Great Britain	Annual
The United Reformed Church Year Book.	United Reformed Church	Annual
Religious Society of Friends' Book of Meetings.	Religious Society of Friends	Annual
The Salvation Army Year Book.	International HQ of the Salvation Army	Annual
The Catholic Directory of England and Wales.	Gabriel Communication	Annual
The Jewish Year Book.	Jewish Chronicle	Annual
UK Christian Handbook.	Marc Europe	

Printed in the UK for HMSO.
Dd294191 c30 7 92